Dangerous Amusements

Ontario Review Press Poetry Series

DANGEROUS AMUSEMENTS

poems by
Jon Davis

Ontario Review Press / Princeton

Copyright © 1985, 1987 by Jon Davis
All rights reserved
Manufactured in the United States of America
First printing 1987

Library of Congress Cataloging in Publication Data

Davis, Jon, 1952–
Dangerous amusements.

(Ontario Review Press poetry series)
I. Title   II. Series
PS3554.A934912D3   1987   811'.54   87-20388
ISBN 0-86538-061-9 (pbk.)

Distributed by Persea Books, Inc.
225 Lafayette St.
New York, NY 10012

ACKNOWLEDGMENTS

I thank the editors of the following journals in which these poems first appeared: *The Bloomsbury Review* ("Darwin," "West Rock," "On the Photographs of Ansel Adams"), *Cedar Rock* ("Touring New England"), *Crosscurrents* ("The Astronaut Remembers His First Space Walk"), *CutBank* ("Perfect Landscapes, Rich Branches of Blossom"), *The Georgia Review* ("That Modern Malice"), *High Plains Literary Review* ("Landscape Assembled from Dreams," "The Sacred"), *Indiana Review* ("The Unmetaphysical Esteves"), *Mid-American Review* ("James Lee Howell, Trucker, Reconsiders His Profession"), *The Minnesota Review* ("Proposition and Lament"), *The Missouri Review* ("Blue Sky, the Girder Falling"), *The Montana Review* ("Breath," "Why I Live on Sutter's Mountain"), *The Ontario Review* ("The Arena of Civilization," "The World," "Grandmother Speaks from Her Chaise Lounge near the Dock," "The Furnace Repairman's Wife," "The Street Preacher Addresses an Audience of the Unruly and the Devout," "Testimony"), *Permafrost* ("The Young Wife"), *Pikestaff Forum* ("Mr. Celentano Remembers the Night Johnny Paris Sang 'Heartbreak Hotel,'" "Note to the Residents of 412 Beechwood Heights"), *Poetry* ("White Body, Green Moss," "Essay on Joy Beginning with Mozart's *Sinfonia Concertante in E flat Major*," "Essay: The Yearbook"), *Poetry Now* ("The Drowning"), *Shankpainter* ("Soteriology," "Downstairs at The Garden Gate Restaurant & Lounge"), *The Silverfish Review* ("Against Sartre"), *Tendril* ("Driving Red Bush Lane"), *Yarrow* ("The Bee Man Removes a Swarm of Honey Bees from under the Eaves of Our House").

A number of these poems—some in earlier versions—appeared in the 1982 Merriam Frontier Award chapbook *West of New England*.

This work was supported by grants from the National Endowment for the Arts and the Fine Arts Work Center in Provincetown. Publication of this work was made possible in part by a grant from the National Endowment for the Arts.

For Terry

CONTENTS

I

*Must every experience—those that promised to be
dearest and most penetrative,—only kiss my cheek
like the wind and pass away?*

> —Ralph Waldo Emerson,
> letter to Caroline Sturgis,
> February 4, 1842

"Perfect Landscapes,
Rich Branches of Blossom"

It is your world to make
and you choose to fill
rooms with necessary objects:
a Chinese vase, a painting of a woman
arranging flowers by moonlight,
a book of poetry by Basho.

A rose leans, revealing its moist stamen
within a halo of fragrance.
Why not a Spanish guitar
leaning in a sunny corner?
Why not music: Villa Lobos
or Rampal and his sentimental flute?

Your women are French, Oriental,
your men—artists, dancers, poets.
Don't you see? Even love
is a luxury. And now you have
cactus blooming in the sun room,
an oriole chirping from the flowering plum.

Someone is quoting Garcia Lorca.
A man wearing white silk,
a woman in a dress of pale cotton:
they sit at a wicker table,
in wicker chairs, looking away,
thinking in image, not word.

In this luxury of sun
they hold crystal goblets
filled with glittering rosé
or thin blood. They kiss,
the nature of their desire revealed
by his restraint, her surrender.

Later, when they make love,
she recalls Nijinsky, turning,

his eyes, his shoulders, softening.
He thinks of Degas: his girlish ballerina
practicing: imagining each smooth stroke
along the flushed inner thigh.

Against Sartre

You begin by refusing the leaves,
the brown leaves of the oak,
last to stutter against branches,
last to fall. Then
you refuse the tree, the sky,
clouds slumped against rock,
the flat-boat
easing through an inlet,
the two fishermen in yellow slickers
facing the sea, imagining nothing—
caught in the routines of joy,
the motions of light and fog,
undulations of water
thick with color: yellow slickers,
the new green of bud and flower,
the slate heron aloft,
trailing its yellow legs.
In this confusion of seasons
these fishermen drift
while you watch from your porch,
the heat clanging in the pipes,
your breath fogging the glass,
the coffee cup steaming in your hand,
wet leaves stuck to your bare feet,
the door left open—warm rain
and the wind. Over the bay
you hear the plunge and stroke
and you know that this
is the edge of an impossible future,
the absence of everything you know.
Over the bay you hear
droplets falling from a stilled oar.

The Sacred

Is not found in the sudden whorl of fingerprints, the
    spider's web, the oyster drill waving its tiny trunk,
    the trumpet worm sunk in silt, its pink fronds
    scything the waves' repetitions—though each
    quickens our longing.

Nor is it found in the inexplicable joy of contrast—the black
    bulk of mountain severed by the red ebullience of the
    sun, the angle a tree makes with slanting ground, a
    white cloud soaking gray stone, the radical enjambment
    of cliff and sky—though this is closer.

Perhaps it emerges when the sea dissolves into a shining,
    when mountain and sun collapse into a single line,
    when rock softens and clouds root deeper, when a web
    becomes slivers of silver light and the oyster drill,
    settling on its prey, begins the tender rasping.

The Spoonbills

—for Terry

The gas lamp built a globe
of white light. Wind roared
in the fire's glass. We huddled close.
Beyond, the nylon tent, inflated, shuddered.
Florida Bay churned into white.
That day, we'd watched black skimmers
make their glittering incisions.
Vultures dipped from the wind
to drink from fountains.
A hawk screamed
from the low plumes of a palm.
The anhinga, pteranodon of the marsh,
clung to a mangrove
and turned, wings fanned in the sun.
Towards evening,
the laughing gulls gathered,
squawking near our tent. Then,
at dusk, the spoonbills flew:
the sun's long last rays reflecting
pink off the soft feathers,
the feathers we knew were soft,
the graceful legs trailing,
the long necks outstretched,
and the flattened bills
we knew but could not see.
What is love? We pointed
and understood.

On the Photographs of Ansel Adams

Grandeur is always the subject: shards
of sunlight splitting clouds; rubble of lost
boulders under a heaven of cliff face and cumuli;
a tiny cemetery—crosses like fence pickets—
near the ghostly town under the mountains
flooding with white, the moon above
like some Platonic ideal. Always this grandeur,
the abstractions light makes beneath
the imperturbable glacier-wrought peaks.
Nothing of the feminine. Always the implied
movement towards perfection. Climax
of will and the willed vision. Always
the mind and the eye and the mind's eye.
The iceberg yielding to the avarice
of gravity. The river at peak flow
and not after. Desert sand brawling
with sunlight and wind. Not delicate may-apple
or seed husk but fulminating surf. Not
the moment but the moment's passing:
the marsh grass, Glacier Bay, '48, bending
and bent with the attentions of rain.

Essay: The Yearbook

Part of the charm of this book—this novel
with too many characters—lies in the repeatability
of the experiment described. Not that each yearbook
replicates the previous year's, but we see how each role
is—more or less—filled: class clown, best-dressed,
most likely to succeed, those who join chess club,
those who take shop, and, always, those who remain
unphotographed. We envy these last, the children
who leave only their names as if to say
We are not a part of this. Whether failures
or revolutionaries is hard to say, our concepts
of *failure* and *revolutionary* being vague
at best, each one melting into the other in such
a society where failure is itself revolutionary,
a rejection of history and culture. But it is
with fondness we recall these deviates, their
unchanging names where their faces might have been,
these fools and outsiders with their leathers or
snap-on ties, drug-bent minds and bleach-blonde
girlfriends from another school who wore too much
makeup and turquoise jewelry, these daughters of alcoholics
and hill men, beautiful in the way all outsiders
are beautiful, the stray dogs who snap and yip
and come, finally, to our hands, the child
who watches us from the far corner, scribbling
with crayons a picture of exactly who we are.

Soteriology

According to the saints, the chosen walk by grace alone
through an obedience prepared for them, as if faith
were a thing granted, not a thing we summon up
within us, a sap willed from the center
of whatever root sustains. Seeing it
their way, nothing can be accomplished. Desire
is a river of sand, a hand sketching a hand
that sketches a hand. In Escher's lithographs,
for example, it is not the pleasure of repetition
he shows us, but the emptiness of reason, how
even as the apes become men we know
that in the kernel of light in which the world
invents itself, they are still apes, and unsaved.
Imagine them in hell, attempts at abstinence
and virtue exchanged for lives of absolute
terror, mouths twisted beyond speech, flames
dripping from their upraised arms.
Even Aquinas, puzzling over such figures,
must have been astonished to hear himself say
that, yes, they were free only to choose their sins,
to choose their seats in the circle of flame.
Knowing this, he must have looked hard
in the eyes of his brothers; he must have thought
All that kindness betrayed by this.
But they are the evil ones, the background
against which the saved prance and celebrate.
So today, in a classroom filled with students
who feign interest, I can envy the young man
who leans his head against the window
and lets his eyelids drop, unconcerned,
uncurious, waiting for the future to swallow him,
to mutter him into a dull simplicity, saving him
at last from this language of need.

The Drowning

A young woman, lithe and anxious, is taking her first man.
Her hair veils her small face.
She laughs. He is somewhere else.
It is noon. They are draining the lake in Westerly.
At the bottom, in the crater of cracked mud, caked
with a fine silt like the victims of Vesuvius, they will find:
a tangle of arms and legs—a young girl huddled against death.
The couple groans, though there is little pain.
They have forgotten wars. They have forgotten the drowned.
They are swimming into each other.
At four o'clock, a uniformed man will lean, drained,
against a stone dam, and stare at the water mark—
3′ 6″—where the body lies, clutched and still.
Other men will be standing nearby, holding cigarettes,
looking away, into the comforting emptiness.

Blue Sky, the Girder Falling

All day long I've been thinking about justice,
that young man from Helena—quarterback, scholar,
wife and young son, the girder falling from the sky . . .
Last week on campus he said we'd beat 'em good this year
and a case of beer was riding on it. I imagine him
kissing his wife good-bye, holding his boy up,
burying his face in the puffy stomach.
Then the long drive north to the work site,
past farmhouses, their windows blazing with sun.
All day long I've been thinking about justice,
the steel falling, Jim Burford smiling, tanned
and shirtless, the yellow hard hat
on the perched shell of his skull. I think
of the crane operator: stories told over beers at Rudy's:
the flask tucked beneath his belt, his wife
unbuttoning her beaded blouse behind the trailer.
All day long I've been thinking about justice.
When it was done they grappled the iron off the body
and the toughest men in Montana looked away.
This afternoon I rake leaves, trying to forgive God.
When I look up at Mount Sentinel I remember
bitterroot blooming in a secret valley,
ticks clinging to the tender slips.
All day long I've been thinking about justice.
Last night, a thunderstorm, lightning
falling in sheets, the muddy river slugging trucks.
I sat with my wife in a car and watched:
pine boughs crashed around us, a ball of lightning
sputtered across the field. My wife
took my hand, kicked open the door.
She walked me into the storm: across
startled suburban lawns, swing sets clanging,
a mutt crashing an aluminum door—whimpering,
the glittering cars, dithering birches,
puddled driveways drenched in light.
All day long I've been thinking about justice,
leaves rushing under the rake, blue sky, the girder falling.

Breath

If it is Tuesday, the fifteenth of June, then the curtains are lifting and wavering in a slight wind. The thin song of an Audubon's warbler rises and falls through the window where a woman is baking bread. The woman's husband runs an edger along the walk, cutting back the sod. He is trying not to think of his mother's death, how she counted herself out of this world.

"One," she'd said, and breathed, and held with both hands to her son's hand, feeling the silver ring carved with a horse's head that he'd worn since he was sixteen. "Two. Three." When she'd reached nine her hands had tightened, then gone limp. This morning, while he was still half-asleep, those hands had come to him, the skin dry and smooth, the fingers bent, the knuckles slick and misshapen. He remembered being afraid to touch that skin, then, unexpectedly, taking her hands. He'd thought she'd smiled then, but he realized later that he'd been mistaken and that what he'd taken for a smile had been an expression without meaning, an expression that signalled the beginning of meaninglessness.

That was Sunday. Today is Tuesday, and he leans to tear a chunk of shelf fungus from the rotting trunk of a dogwood, a tree he'd meant to cut down last fall until he'd discovered the hole and, inside the hole, the nest lined with pale blue and orange down. The odor of the fungus is, he thinks, sharp and sexual, unlike the smell of baking bread that he thinks of as feminine and not sexual but gracefully erotic, as when he watches his wife at her tea, absorbed in the play of sunlight along the blonde hairs of her arms. When he stands, the smell of baking bread blows past him, and he sees his wife through the gauze curtains. He thinks that she is older now, and that he is older. He thinks that he and his brothers are all that's left of their mother, and he feels diminished.

Since Sunday they have done nothing but make arrangements—they chose the coffin, picked out clothes that she might have worn had this been her sister's funeral and not her own, and wrote an obituary notice for the local newspaper. He'd wanted to say something grand about his mother, but found there was nothing he could say. She'd been a good mother, undistinguished except by idiosyncracies whose pleasures were private and arose from repetition—how she would answer

13

the phone so cheerfully when her children called from college that it seemed she knew they were about to call, how, later, she'd watch football on television, cheering so loudly at touchdowns that someone would inevitably rush into the room to be sure she hadn't fallen.

He knew that reading these facts in the newspaper would not make them more true. He knew that the agony of all this would pass, that the warbler singing in the cedar was simply marking his territory, that that was the only meaning, that beauty was incidental. He breathed deeply. Bread, grass, his mother's hands, the curtains blowing, his wife's quick motions behind the kitchen window—all of it was in the air. He felt it. It filled him. He breathed again.

Landscape Assembled from Dreams

The lake under mist like an eye, opening,
a disc of light adrift among the drawn
shadows of pines, quivering hemlocks
pressed tight to the tensed surface.
Three boys move on the cliff face, down
into the stroke of sunlight pushing
through mist, slashing a single vein of light
across the basaltic spires. In this
plausible light, green deepening to blue,
air thick with moisture, with the smells
of fern and moss, of leaf mold, the boys walk,
revising this landscape assembled from dreams,
the drift of intelligence stilling each sequence
as it occurs—the hawk pinned to the sky,
the single cry that quickens stone,
the lake suddenly clear and without detail,
the hawk gone, the boys stepping back
into their separate lives.

Touring New England

In New England tourists curve through towns
on slick pavement. Every bend brings
new gusts of weather. Here the sun shines
and women—tanned and made grave
by summers at the Cape—stride among
the keen details of landscape:
cottages thrust against sea and sky,
waves rummaging through gravel.
Such steady pressures carve this place:
the men stream from factories
where the least error makes the blood
go hollow, or ride to work six to a car
not noticing the shoreline recede,
the wreckage fouling their rivers.
Generations here are united by granite,
cut, polished, thrust up
into new formations. Whole walls
of sunlight stun the cities. Tourists
gape at the horizon, cluttered
by cloud and spray, water too cold to swim,
or trudge through heat to purchase schooners
and stuffed seals, landscapes made
of surf and surface. They return
to Kansas or Missouri where neighbors gawk
at the shapes attained by sand,
the gull's awkward flights,
a sailboat tilted beyond belief.

Essay on Joy Beginning with Mozart's
Sinfonia Concertante in E flat Major

Imagine Mozart in the warm haze of his gift blurting
Melody is simple! then sitting at the piano to improvise
a dozen. It is as if Einstein, over coffee,
were to casually mention relativity, the curved space/time
continuum, and quantum mechanics for the first time
while poking dully at his coffee ring or glancing
at a feeder where goldfinches and sparrows
have just landed. Or those *idiot savants*, twin brothers,
who would call out ten-digit primes, then eleven, twelve,
speaking in a language so pure and full of delight
it cannot be translated, like the glossolalia
which seems the voice of Satan, but which
must taste like rich and richly textured
pastries, or the cool taste of wet wind
in a dry mouth. Joy is not
what we think. Nor is it a result of anything
in particular—gift of melody or insight, numbers
arriving from an inarticulate distance . . .
it must fall equally to those who toil
over the simplest task, the scowling
sixty-year-old man who crosses
and recrosses the laces of his black shoes
until they finally attain a pattern he knows,
clear as sunlight cutting a broth
of clouds and fog, a theme restated,
shrill piccolo through a ravishment of strings.

That Modern Malice

*So you get all them weird chords which don't mean
nothing, and first people get curious about it just
because it's new, but soon they get tired of it because
it's really no good and you got no melody to remember
and no beat to dance to. So they're all poor again and
nobody is working, and that's what that modern malice
done for you.*

—Louis Armstrong

Listen: a rose lynched in the arbor,
a honeybee frisking the orchid's heart:
variations on a theme. Not lovers
murmuring near sleep, the rituals of love
completed in the room next to yours,
not that kind agreement to deceive,
but this: a purity rising in your throat,
just the truth—how you looked in her eyes
and thought for no reason of car lights
drifting over the bridge into Manhattan,
or the nameless future that draws all of us
to the edge of madness or drink, then
turns without a word and plays the chorus straight,
the way a tree full of crows purifies the heart.
The way you walk alone on a city night
past bars alive with smoke and noise
where the neon snap and buzz plays every memory,
your heart punching you on into the heartless solo.
Desire is not a concentration of fact,
but a glissando, a sudden modulation,
snatch of "Melancholy Baby"
in the midst of "Yardbird Suite."
No moment is big enough, and when you
break into the chorus, even the comping piano
chafes like a woman on the phone,
like the rhythm of paycheck to paycheck,
show from nine to three, dress codes and charts.
Each note is a history of itself,
an embolus rising to the brain. Listen:
a honeybee drones in the orchid's heart.

II

*We may come to think that nothing
exists but a stream of souls, that
all knowledge is biography.*
                    —William Butler Yeats

Proposition and Lament

This child that wobbles from living room
to kitchen wearing his diaper, his fat legs
blotched with pink, his hair twisted into peaks,
babbles a language all syntax, like
birdsong or the rhetoric of hounds,
while I sit in my thirteen-year-old's clothes,
novice at fashion, at not being different,
at not drawing attention, at being stupid
like the rest of my thirteen-year-old world.
The child's mother waves her dry, white-skinned
arms and chain-smokes menthol cigarettes
where she sits at the black-and-white specked
formica table. I'm too young to understand
any of this, but I listen to a story of abandonment
and sin, doors slammed, an all-night bus trip
from West Virginia, some lust that pries a man
from a woman and sends her into the corner
of her brain where speech is backed up
on an assembly line one part against another,
saying nothing. I listen to the child
and the mother speak this language
of avoidance, of deference and sigh. In one hour
I'll go to school and learn to hate what makes us true,
to snub the lonely and the poor, the mad
who know something suddenly and can't say what it is—
an idea, or a feeling, or the ghost of a feeling.
I'll wear the same pair of jeans all week, the same
stupid shirt everyone wears. I'll speak
the same language filled with the flash of chrome,
verbs like gemstones, nouns big and plural as cadillacs,
adjectives that print foreheads.
I'll walk around behind my eyes taking everything
that's given. I'll pledge allegiance, line up
behind the future. I'll come home, lie awake, and listen
to the boy shaking his crib, his mother
tapping ashes into a half-filled coke bottle by the bed.

The Young Wife

Once I walked here whistling the sparrow's song,
arranging porcelain figures on the windowsill
and spinning the wind chimes. I heard swallows
breathe clouds of twittering song, a cat purring,
a jazz guitar. Now I watch grosbeaks
lurch like rodents in the cottonwoods, a robin—
puffed-up, violent—perched stiff as a thumb.
The man who walks through the gate is wild-eyed
and gestures at trees and vines. He speaks
a language of grunts and sighs and belittles the cat.
His mouth grows slack, like an infant's. Nights
I lie in bed and listen to him clicking his 21 channels.
What kind of world is this that promises so much?
Our yard grows wild. I don't ask him to mow or trim.
I don't look him in the eye. At dinner he mentions
the plumbing, or work. When he leaves
he kisses my face good-bye. Last night
he stayed out until dawn. All night I waited,
listening to the wisteria—grown thick
as a man's arms—as it grappled with shingles,
twisting and creaking, thatching the windows and doors.

Grandmother Speaks from Her Chaise Lounge near the Dock

You boys could give us
a thrill once in a while, something
to set this day apart
from the others stacked behind us
like dominoes ready to fall. Soon,
my heart will be a white line
on a scope; it will sing
a single note
in the white room of my brain.
So give us a thrill, a skier
upside down
in these bushes by the dock,
a near collision of these fancy boats,
a boy tangled in the ropes,
dragged like a log
through the hard water.
Let's see a boat
tipped up on its side
until all that fancy hardware
falls out like the soul
falls out of the body.
And why not whip a skier
through the shallows—
a big man, a smart-ass
when he loses one ski,
when he sends it skidding
to where it just nicks
that young girl's forehead.
Then bring her here
so I can touch the spot
where the blood pulses out
from the temple,
so I can rock her
and listen to her cry.

The Astronaut Remembers
His First Space Walk

—after Dick Allen

As you walk in the long present,
boots on gravel,
the branch-ends of the mimosa
like feathers, the pink flowers,
even in moonlight, like tropical birds
perched and trembling, you remember
floating in light, the cord unraveling,
one stone white, the other blue,
swathed in vapors, and the surprise—
nearly alone, one line tethering you
to the craft—you were only yourself,
the past like a stone, a ballast
to your life, and you remembered
oatmeal, your grandmother, sunlight
falling through glass, and how you
placed your hand into that liquid
and thought of honey, and bees
swarming over the lawn—a cloud of bees—
and all the children called inside
watching at the windows as bees
buzzed and battered glass, and you turned
to see your mother standing alone
in the exact center of the room,
her face pale, drawn, beautiful.

A Couple from Kentucky Witness the Rocky Mountains at Dusk

Fifty feet straight down, the river trembles with light.
The woman moves her hands to frame shades of blue and red.
A lone cloud—puffed and virtuous, ruminative—
grazes the orange face of a cliff. "Georgia
O'Keeffe," she says. "Only Georgia O'Keeffe
could make that real." And clear as agate.
Beautiful, meaningless: the code of the eye
broken into shades of blood and bone.

Her husband's fingers pry at clips
and latches, coax legs from their metal sleeves.
He watches light fail on the purple mountains.
She speaks with a voice like wind rushing over stone.
He snaps each section of leg into place. "Kentucky,"
she says, "was never like this."
Light nests in the cirque.
Darkness coddles the lake.

Her husband bolts the camera in place.
She will remember colors, cool air
blowing up from the canyon—unpaintable
darkness, indefinite sadness, a river
too far from its source. Tonight,
while she sleeps, moonflowers will open:
damp petals fluttering in moonlight. But now
her husband frames the scene; the camera clicks.

Overhead, a blue heron strokes towards its nest,
silken wings rustling, legs trailing,
each toe visible, each joint a delicate bud.

Darwin

A victim of thought,
you fall asleep to happy novels.
You propose these laws: happy ends
for every book, at least one character
no one could hate. In New York
old Agassiz walks with God along the cases,
naming: each species distinct,
enclosed in mahogany and glass.
Tomorrow, he sails for Tierra del Fuego
and the finches of Galápagos.
Looking on those islands
he will lean against the rigging,
pull his greatcoat close,
and close his eyes.
One year from death,
he will see God's plan revealed:
"Had it been otherwise,
there would be nothing but despair."
Charles, you did what you could.
You'd written his son:
"Pray give my most sincere
respects to your father.
What a wonderful man. . . ."
You are sorry to have made
this world without purpose.
You question your own morality.
Why can you no longer find
pleasure in human works—
in art and music, in poetry?
You'd planned on the ministry:
the phrenologist had moved his hands
like spiders over the bumps of faith.
"Enough for three men!" he pronounced.
You sailed for Galápagos instead.
There you saw your finches
honed by time and weather.
There you learned the meaning of Pele's tears:
small monuments to heavenly sadness,
iridescent droplets of basalt.

"Look," your father said
as you hoisted your journals
and peered over the rail at Falmouth,
"even the shape of his head has changed!"

The Bee Man Removes a Swarm of Honey Bees from under the Eaves of Our House

Who's been stung so often he brags,
"Poison makes me strong!" Claims a heart
that hums and flutters, won't start
without the cash in hand. He drags
a suit and mask from the back of the van,
leans a makeshift ladder against the porch,
speaks in German to the queen. "Meine Liebe, much
you've got to learn," he says. "Come home,
come home, each thing will be all right."
He eyes us where we cower behind the storm door
feeling the needle-prick of air that swarms
beneath our shirts. "They say a bee's like a man—a slight
to bees," he says, "who work as hard as immigrants,
hum a little hymn, die old and ignorant."

The Unmetaphysical Esteves

—after Fernando Pessoa

The unmetaphysical Esteves
has a new plan: he will
memorize the states and
their capitals, learn
to wiggle his ears, teach
himself to write backwards,
set a new pogo-stick record,
time himself coming home
from work, find out which
is faster: highway or back
roads, learn to recognize
cars by their grilles.

The unmetaphysical Esteves
has found a pipe tobacco
that doesn't bite, he's
saving box tops, knows
all three MVPs
with the number 32.
He wants to invent
a hot-seat for football games,
a flask that looks like a book.
He's got a new computer watch;
he's adding it up.
Look at that smile.

James Lee Howell, Trucker, Reconsiders His Profession

Cows are dumb as clay and these
the dumbest I'd seen, wide-eyed
and oblivious on the two-lane bridge.

At three a.m., such sights are common—
you might jerk the wheel some night
and pass right through a ton of beef.

But not this time. Imagine a Volkswagen
made of beef. Imagine a dream that is
not a dream. Imagine the slugfest

when my bumper socked those cows
and my rig shuddered and pitched
and slammed the steel guardrail. Then

it was headlights veering
like spotlights, a sheet
of sparks, and a sound

like the lowing of cows in a stockyard
who know they are meat and have always
been meat despite the pleasant

futureless days of grazing. Then I was rolling,
clothes, pens, books floating past me,
the CB—miles away—busting with static.

I thought then, right then, that I
was dumb as clay, my wide eyes
blotted out, and a wife somewhere

beyond any voice I might have mustered.

West Rock

From the flats of Woodbridge it rises now
what never rose but stayed as memories stay.
When I was ten my father drove me
to these sheer sienna cliffs, blue sky;
my fearless brother leaned to look
at two men hanging from a ledge.
I thought they'd die before they reached the top;
I saw the fall through air, the clutch
at nothing, the knowing body turned
to face the talus slope. In a movie, once,
I'd seen a man, an extra really,
his chest torn wide by a shotgun blast.
When he saw the ragged hole they'd painted
on his chest, the blood and bits of flesh
they'd splattered in his lap, he mouthed
the words "my god," and I knew
that if he played it right he must then think
of what he'd done that day—the turn he'd made
from Church to Grove, the cup of coffee
he'd refused that made him fifteen minutes
early for his work and prompt for his demise.
I watched my father while he sat and smoked
on a bench beside Three Judges' Cave,
that clump of boulders fenced with steel bent wide
to let the winos and the high-school kids
smash bottles and paint their names and dates.
I wondered what turn he'd made wrong to turn
a marriage into nothing, into air
you couldn't grab. He held a Pall Mall tight
between his lips and watched his hands—I see it
now—as that movie man had watched his chest.
I sat beside him then; he put one hand
down on my shoulder, jostling me,
then pulled my head against his chest—
his rings that scraped against my head,
the smell of smoke. He took
a plastic bag out of his pocket,
opened it and spilled the balsa wood.
He fit the parts together on the bench

31

to make a plane. He held it up
for me to see. "How's that?" he said.
It was beautiful; I told him that. We walked
past an older couple sitting on a bench—
the woman held her husband's hands
flat against her lap; neither
moved nor spoke. We stopped
on the brown cliff's edge—some stunted,
brittle-looking scrub, a sheer rock wall,
the valley floor. He held me while I threw.
We watched it soar, turn, flutter, and
fall as those two men would fall,
their rope pulled taut, then slackening,
as they drifted far, or near enough to touch.

Downstairs at The Garden Gate
Restaurant & Lounge

Sunday again, and a hard rain blows
against red brick and trashcans,
                    gusting against the Oldsmobile
sunk in its gray sadness,

and the windows multiplying skyward . . .

Sunday, and the man sags
lower under his burden—
                    his wife's accusing face
each morning of his failure,
how he sits all day addressing a mirror—

he remembers '69, an autumn day, cool,
a breeze scattering leaves,
                    his teenaged son
dropping back to throw a pass,
his own awkward lunge,

the football slapping off his hands . . .

*

Not *madness*
                  with its bottles smashed in the alley,
not *grief* with its flakes of rust in the tap water.

(For hours he thinks of Crown Street,
the theater there,
                  seats of crimson felt and the curtain lifting,
a cone of flecked light parting the dark.
On Sundays, after the movie,
                  he and his wife tossing popcorn
to addled pigeons and fierce gulls,
their son at home, sleeping
                  under a mobile touched
by his slow breathing, the babysitter
kissing her boyfriend in the next room.

33

                Later,
the chunks of concrete and iron spikes
strewn in vacant lots,
the pigeons flicking their stubborn wings
above the women with their shopping bags,
                                the sleeping drunks,
while office workers swung into their cabs,
he and his wife, on the bridge, the river surging
through the bent frames of shopping carts,
February sun a single spike through a break
in the low clouds,
                time stuck in the river's throat,
in the wink and gasp of the sun-struck windows . . .)

There is no word for any of this, nor
for the dumb river of light
washing over the glittering screen.

                                *

It's not cash or no cash,
                        not love's eye gleaming,
but always beyond this dailiness,
routines of hurt and forgiveness, the laundry
flung in the closet, the television's needle
                        deep in his brain . . .

                                *

Sometimes, when the buildings close off the sky as they do now,
        so surely,
and nighthawks *beep*, and slash their wings
                        through the high windows' faint light,
the bars close,
                and men and women
huddle in cars, the engines running,
and warm their hands over defrosters,
nobody around to shake their shoulders until they wake
                                in their childhood beds.

Some nights are longer than life,
the son dead in a white room
                              in another state,
as though carved in marble,
and a country song whose melody
                    won't fit the words
until the nurse clicks it off and the doctor,
unprofessionally,
                   strokes the slack wrist.

Some nights are longer than life,
when a mockingbird creaks and chatters
                    refusing to be emblem or symbol,

and his wife rises from bed, gathering her robe, and listens,
as a confused pleasure drives through her flesh,
to the telephone's small voice,
                    the curve of words, the tree and the flames,
her son, the idea of her son.

                              *

He wants to stand on the bridge
            in darkness, in rain,
and see something adrift on the water—a light—
            and point with his son's hand.

                              *

This is the night when the tankers and barges ride
low in the hurricane tide,
                    when the black crude in the hulls
is memory, and the harbor, like the horizon, recedes.

Fifteen years, and he remembers Gulf Beach, the breakwater,
whitecaps, and eels thrashing in the shallows,
how they beat them on the rocks . . .

So he has come here,
the bartender snapping bottles off the shelves,
                              the phone waking him
to another dream,

         his wife cutting back roses in the cold rain,
with no thought to her sagging print dress, her bare feet
sunk in mud; around her face,
the coarse hair
         hanging like moss.

III

Unless all existence is a medium for revelation,
no revelation is possible.

—William Temple

Note to the Residents
of 412 Beechwood Heights

We don't take much—the ten records you got
for ninety-nine cents, a jar of pennies,
your teenaged daughters' diaries. We've seen
enough television to know the tricks—
a flashlight taped until one line of light
seeps into the room, dark gloves, ski hats,
sneakers blackened with magic markers.
The footprints we leave outside your porch
are smooth, without direction. We X your glass
with tape, crack it with a flannel-wrapped hammer.

Last week we watched from behind the hedge
while you undressed, your bodies glowing
in the lamplight. Now, we walk this well-
imagined route from porch to kitchen
to bedroom, fanning the light's thin beam
over jars filled with flour, sugar and tea, over
snapshots and keys, a list of the miles you've run.
We don't take much—a bottle of whiskey,
a letter you left on the counter. In the bedroom
we find gold earrings on the night stand,
a silk gown my brother swears he saw you drop.

We stand at the window and look out at the hedge
shaken by something we don't quite know . . .
We don't take much—a water-stained copy
of *Peyton Place*, a stack of *Playboys*: these secrets
are safe with us. We stand in the kitchen
and watch headlights flare against the blinds,
hear every sound—a dog barking two houses down,
a garage door rolling open, the alarm clock
ticking beside the bed. Tonight
your daughters will undress in our dreams,
and nothing you can say will call them home.

Those Dying Generations

It began last Sunday, or—if truth be told—
Began ten weeks ago when we moved in. My wife
Works north, in Naugatuck; I write for *The Bridgeport Post*.
We chose this valley town to split the drive.
But ten weeks now the woman who shares
The ground floor with her forty-year-old daughter
Has wheezed and whined that ingrate daughter's sins.
Ten weeks now they have drummed their goddamn anger
Against the stairway wall. "Such is the torment,"
I tell my wife, "five bills a month
Can buy these days." I'm a reasonable man; my wife
More reasonable still. When irrationality
Is required, she relies on me.

Sunday last, I stirred my whiskey sour with my finger,
Sucked it clean, sat on our second-story porch.
The daughter wheeled her mother out
Next to the garage, lifted her—
Hands under both her arms—and set her
Bouncing in a green, spring-steel chair,
Hands flopping in her lap, a particolored
Afghan spread across her thighs.
The mother watched the ground awhile, then
Raised her head to screech some childish
Nonsense. Or perhaps she made some sense;
The daughter seemed to think so. My wife was out
Taking photographs of our new shopping mall.

She's a journalist, a photojournalist,
Which means she's eying you and me
And hoping—in the name of art—
For public mutilation. I thought of her
On Sunday when those two women—mother nearly
Dead, a victim of the constant pain she'd wanted;
Daughter tangled in her mother's dreams for her—
Turned to almost face each other.
And then they nearly spoke. I framed that scene
That seemed to speak, obliquely, of some great
And human failure—white garage, a pear tree,
Bed of pachysandra, the concrete walks
From house to shed, garbage neatly bagged and stacked.

The daughter shook her head. The mother kicked.
The daughter gestured to the house
As if it were some miles away. The mother
Stomped her feet. The daughter sat down on the stoop
And wrapped her arms about her knees.
I was about to pour another drink, but stopped.
I watched the mother's face scrunch up,
The water pool, then run along the drive.
The daughter yelled and fussed
And waved her arms. The mother stared.
Like a child, she watched as though
What was running down the drive was nothing
She had done, was, in fact, some act of God.

The daughter rose and stomped into the house. The screen door
Screeched and slammed. The mother
Watched the urine flow toward Maple Street.
Something in her face—some mindless glee—made me
Turn away. I went inside and made my drink and heard
The daughter's music—loud, a big-band tune, a bland
Romance, a crooner coming nearer polka
Than to swing. I thought right then
Of Coltrane playing Truth, the bitter truth, his
Face turned to the wall, and those famous
Starving Sikhs in '47, who—though dying—
Marched and posed three hours for Bourke-White.
She might have said, "Let's see more bone

And bloated stomach." After all, she had
A Pulitzer to win. And win she did. And yet
That photograph confers some grace—Sikhs
In their stately, staggered death waltz,
Captured calmly in their fates. It lends
Their suffering magnitude. And that is all
We ask. All, perhaps, we ever ask. Those Sikhs
Bourke-White froze in a fine despair
Gave me a luscious feeling, but it passed.
But now I see more clearly that old woman
In her chair: old and sick, the night's cold
Settling down, a cold mist raised—the indefinite,
Sad beauty of a Monet. A way of looking that

Could force a quiet corner in the warring world.
A week ago, that was. My wife will not
Forgive my watching. It was she who called
The ambulance at midnight. The daughter's music
Gently filtered through the ducts. Red lights
Flashed across our faces. Officially, I'd
Been reading and had the stereo up.
"I'm not much," I told the driver, "for snooping
On the neighbors." I laughed a little
There; my wife coughed and looked away.
The woman nearly died, but made it. I insist
She wanted it that way. Her daughter hovers now
Like a vulture over her (a visual simile—

Her head hangs forward—but there's truth
Inside that sight). Yesterday, I
Told my wife that it could have been
Much worse—I might have had a camera. She scoffed,
But I recalled her fellow journalist
Who won prizes for his sequence of a man
Who'd caught a sniper's shot while wheeling boxes
Past a store. The first photo shows the man
Stumbling to his van, pleading to the camera,
Trailing blood behind him on the street. He's driving
In the second shot, but swerving towards a car.
By the third, he's smashed into a stanchion,
And banging wide the door—now this

Is why the sequence won awards—he
Falls, clutching at the steering wheel, and dies.
Or how about, I said, that gallery of photographs
We spent one Sunday in. The pale, puffy body
Of the murdered boy, face up, his mouth
A kind of hopeful blossom under water;
That shape repeated artfully in
The wound's ironic smile. The boy's
Hand across his eyes as though made
Bashful by something said, too intimate.
Okay. I'll say it straight: I
Despised that woman and her daughter.
And though I never wished them ill, I

Let them have their ills. It seemed
A small thing to indulge them in their pettiness,
Since pettiness is what their lives have been. And
Had the mother died? Not much to change.
The daughter'd dance her screwy waltz
To Mantovani, Lawrence Welk. She'd walk
To Tony's Market every Tuesday noon, her head
Wrapped in a scarf. I suppose she'd have been
Lonely and regretted what she'd done.
I'd have been relieved (not openly)
To have just music climb our stairs.
But after all this talk, I'm left with this:
Each night my wife brings home her job

As if it were another man with his demands.
She'll wake and sit straight up in bed
And cry *Look out!* then pat the sheets
As if to find a lens. And it occurs to me
What irked me most about her friend
Was not his prize, but that dry champagne
We shared at forty bucks a throw, the joy we'd wrought
So far beyond that blood-encrusted day,
The way he raised his glass to toast the prize
And our complicity—not to spoil his
Momentary joy—in clicking glass to glass.
My wife moved to the couch last Sunday night.
A week had passed; she'd slept there ever since.

Last night, I half awoke and, waking further, thought
I'd heard a stifled sobbing in the bath, or heard
A suitcase packed and finally shut. I felt as much as
Saw the wash of light that was my wife's
Warm body in the middle of our room.
Softly, with an unbearable resolve, she said
Or seemed to say, "I'm leaving you." And that
Threat, coming out of sleep and silence, coming
After hours of darkness, a voice controlled,
Stretched tight across the drum of grief,
Sounded sweet and warm. I stood, walked to her.
We touched, trembling, and began to sway
In a kind of slow and aimless waltz.

The Street Preacher Addresses an Audience of the Unruly and the Devout

Friends, I used to drink like a fish but now He calms my hand.
He speaks to me in tongues, a tiny voice
like a honeybee trapped in a tulip,
but I hear him loud and clear.
And, brothers and sisters, it fortifies me.
I'm ready to do anything,
even call my mother who will drop
into hell like a fat red coal
despite all my good intentions.
Because she won't hear me when I tell her
she's only a vessel, that I'm delivered
of her womb into the Lord's.
She won't listen to John 3:16:
clear as a jar of lead-free,
it sets a fire in my heart.

The Lord is easy as multiplication.
He stands up in my brain and hums
and I know that one night He'll come down,
suck the breath from her lips,
and I'll have lost her forever.
This troubles me deeply.
So I tell her the parable of the night,
the dark night of the soul.
Her soul, the pit of a prune
until she hears the voice in the darkness,
the voice that is a light, that is
the entrance ramp to the freeway of salvation,
the salvation and the eternal life. Such
are the ways of the Lord, such
is the mystery. And He is real.

Friends, He is real as the bloated stomachs
of African children waving flies away
on late night TV, real
as the bottles that clatter past my feet
when I preach in front of K Mart,

when I call forth the sinners
in their corrective shoes,
with those quick eyes that would swallow me
into their need. I am not an educated man,
but His voice pours through me;
my tongue falls asleep and wakes
a strange animal, howling
of *the purifying flame of the Lord.* Such
are the wonders of the Lord, such
are His works. That a man like me

could stand on this filthy sidewalk
and deliver a sermon blazing
with big words and the names of apostles
while buses groan and whine
and jackhammers rap against pavement.
But I am not, as Christ was not, loved.
The teenagers come out of Video World
in their T-shirts and leather jackets
to bark like the dogs of hell, throw
lit cigarettes and bottles at my feet.
But God will damn them to float
on their tender backs in a pool of fire.
Damn them to a hell much like
the one they waste their Saturdays in—
behind everything they see,

an evil logic. A logic I speak against daily.
Hear me: Our souls are butterflies
closed in this city's hands, this city
whose veins pump liquor
through the drunk man's heart, whose voice
babbles from a thousand black boxes. This city
where buses spew the lost and ignorant
into the underground mall
to clothe their bodies and fill their minds
until nothing they say
can touch what they once were. . . .
But the Lord will damn them as he once
damned me, to swim upward
through an amber liquid towards a wafer
of light so thin and distant

I thought my body was a weight and longed
to be rid of it: the hands that thought
bad thoughts, the mouth that suckled
like a piglet the glass teat, the voice
that flopped like a toad from my mouth.
Friends, one morning I woke and saw my ghost
sleeping beside me in the window
of what I later learned was the K. of C.
and I knew I was alone and dying.
I walked to Sears thinking *white, white, white,*
counting my footsteps because they wanted
counting. Between a hockey game
and a movie of four young men
who could not play their instruments,
I saw a man weeping because the Lord

had paid his rent. Such is the mystery,
I now know, of the Lord. Such are His works.
I felt something move on my heart
like a school of minnows, like whiskey
steaming through flesh. When the salesman
asked me to leave I knew what I should say.
"The Lord will take you into His arms,"
I said, "and kiss you full on the mouth,
and you will live forever." I felt
a huge weight unbuckled and lifted
from my shoulders. I felt a thin man
begin knocking kewpie dolls down
with a softball somewhere far back
in the carnival of my brain. Such
are the mysteries of the Lord. Such

are His works. Now I preach daily
to the congregation of the Five-and-Dime.
They are the ones I would live
forever with—the women with both hands
on their purses, the men with their
coat-pocket flasks. They stand
in their glass booths, picking their feet
up and putting them sadly back down.
They understand that these bodies are plaster;
they feel it flaking and falling.

They hear me when I tell them
the secret of their deaths. They push
their glasses back up onto their noses;
they cough into their fists. I can see them
already in heaven, laughing

in their new bodies of music and glass.
And they are grateful, grateful
the way my mother is not. Sometimes
I feel the Lord sink so deeply
in my heart that I am prepared
to tear all of this down for Him,
ready to begin the new flood, the flood
of fire, and I see so clearly
what must be done—the jars and jars
of gasoline, the rags dipped in,
wrung dry. . . . A sacrament
to burn the longing from their hearts,
to make them pure as they once were
and can be again if they will fall
as I have, into the arms of the Lord.

Testimony

"I want to take this time so 'generously' given
by the court to tell you of my genius for
destruction, the drugs that slide like honey
through my veins, the nights I've spent with
women you can't even dream of—the model who
crashed our Labor Day picnic with her hand-
shaking boyfriend, who left and came back
alone at two a.m. to take her dress off and
lie down in Tony's van . . . That was my life
until some idiot baby-faced hero jumped from
behind a wall and I pulled my piece. And
blew him backwards to nowhere, and past that
to where the devil picked his heart up like
a magazine, flipped the pages of his life, hissed
like a blown piston, and tossed it on the fire
if you believe the crap they hand you . . ."

That's not what he said, the man who killed Larry Johnson (who
bowled on my uncle's Thursday night bowling team), the man who
lived with a friend of mine named Jack until Jack decided to move
out because "You hang around with guys like that too long and pretty
soon you're in trouble, too." So now Jack paints houses and tries not
to drink too much and every once in a while he remembers his life
with Lisa, how he chose the only direction he could, and chose wrong.
He feels sorry for the guy on my uncle's bowling team who lived
down the street from my wife's father's house and never did anything
wrong, but had a half-sister who stole a bag of cocaine from a man
with a .38 and a quick finger because "If you led the life I lead you'd
understand I had to kill any man who turned a corner or came down
the stairs like that." So now he's in prison while the guy on my uncle's
bowling team is dead, and my friend who lived with a murderer
paints houses, and my uncle continues to bowl, holding a 200 average
in several leagues. I can't say I feel anything for the dead man. And
I can't stop thinking about the man who pulled the trigger. But what
I wrote is not what he said, the man who killed a man on my uncle's
bowling team. The reporters asked him what he thought of the life
sentence, and he said, "I thought it was a good sentence. A damn

good sentence. I'm getting a warm place to sleep and a good hot meal. Larry Johnson's dead in his grave and I'm getting free room and board. What do I think of the sentence? I think it sucks, you stupid assholes." Then he pushed the microphones away and sang "The worms crawl in, the worms crawl out." Then they took him away.

Driving Red Bush Lane

I've got my own way, see,
I don't want to live like my father—
thirty years in a sweatshop
then one day you're fishing
beers out of a tub of ice
with the whole family jabbering
and flinging lawn darts and your heart
just swells and bursts.
I know, I saw it all.
And my mother,
her face went flooey—eyes
wide and darting. She looked at me
like I could fix it, then
watched the whole thing, moaning,
"Jimmy, Jimmy." She just watched,
just watched him
in front of the whole damn family
and me just a kid, what could I do?

I could've played basketball;
I can handle the ball, shoot
ten-for-ten from the top of the key.
My father knew the coach of Notre Dame;
I could've gotten a scholarship.
But then he went and he died.
It pisses me off sometimes
to see other kids and their fathers.
I hear them in the stands saying,
"Protect the ball with your body,"
or yelling, "Three seconds"
when I'm standing in the lane.
No, I'm through with sports.
I've got my own way now,
my own plans. I'll learn to
drive a semi, join the Guard, maybe
pick up the guitar again. There's
a lot of things I could do.

Saturdays I spend waxing my Camaro.
I pop Black Sabbath into the tape deck
and all the kids ride down on their bikes
to listen and help clean. This
is the fastest car in The Valley—bar none.
It's got an Edelbrock Hi-Rise Manifold
with a big old Holly Four Barrel
squatting right on top
pissing gas into that motor
faster than an elephant. Yeah,
I've got my own way.
I don't like to be bothered. My mother
comes nosing around here sometimes
on weekends. But I don't let her in my room,
I don't tell her nothin'. She checks
my tires for wear, but what's she know?
I tell her it's normal. "These tires," I say,
"they're soft rubber—for traction—they wear down."

But I tear 'em up on Red Bush Lane,
alongside the railroad tracks. I carve J's
all over that road and the kids go wild.
No one's ever seen a driver like me—
I'm a little different, I like to take a chance.
Some nights I'll run that whole goddamn road
without lights. All three miles. Last week,
driving like that, I hit something.
I felt it thud against the bumper.
The car shook and jumped. It sent us
skidding, but it felt good—
like crushing a berry under your boot.
Like I said, I've got my own way.
We turned around—Crazy Joey and me—
and went back to see what we hit.
We went past it once, fast, and Joey,
well, he said it was a dog.
But I saw it good, and I know.

But I didn't say nothin', just drove.
Drove fast enough that neither of us
had time to think—not about what we hit,
or what's right and what's wrong,

51

or about my father, dying like a fool
in front of the whole family.
We closed The Frog Pond that night.
The series was on, Joey got drunk,
Jackson hit another homer. I had a friend
hung himself in the halfway house
across from The Pond. I used to
whip his ass on the asphalt courts
back of Beaver Street School. Lately,
I think about those games, how,
with the score nineteen to one,
I'd drive the lane and jam it, or,
in a close game, I'd rock back on my heels
and nail a twenty-footer. What did I want?

Home from The Pond, I stood in the driveway
until three-thirty just looking at my car—
how the moonlight glittered in the chrome,
curved along the windshield. I listened
to cars rushing on the highway; twice
I heard sirens. I know what I've done,
but I'm young—I've got a life to live.
In the morning I washed the car,
walked to The Hiway Diner for coffee.
I didn't look at the papers, not even *The News*
spread out on the counter—a picture
of some woman who killed her doctor husband.
Only I know, maybe Joey but he won't say.
Later I walked the fire roads through
Water Company land and looked down on Red Bush Lane:
two cops cruising, then, for no reason,
flooring it past the torn garbage bags, tool sheds,
stacks of railroad ties, their 440s howling . . .

Today, for the first time in a week,
I stopped at the courts, shot baskets
with the gang. Chuck's van
was pulled up close, the tape player
blasting. There was a girl there
used to be in my home room. I drove her
to school once and she said
she'd seen me play basketball

and she thought I was good. I remember her eyes
looking at me through her brown hair.
I think I'd like to go see her, to talk
about those games on Beaver Street, maybe
go for a ride up the River Road, past Newtown
and Sharon, past the lake where Joey keeps his boat,
the dam, past The Crossroads Diner,
farther than I've ever needed to go. . . .
I don't want to live like my father, that's
not my way. I've got something better in mind.

Mr. Celentano Remembers the Night Johnny Paris Sang "Heartbreak Hotel"

I'm not proud of what I did. I'd rather
not have made the choice. But Johnny Paris
came in here dressed like Elvis and bothered
the band all night, as if to dare us

to do something. Paris is no stranger—
let's get that straight. He's a drunk
as far as I know, a scavenger
left over from the wars. You'd think

we'd take better care of boys like that—
all shot up and worse—trying to collect
what we owe them. Don't think I forgot
about that. I lost a brother. That's a debt

no one can pay. So Paris comes in here,
wants to sing. He's not bad actually.
Could maybe make a go of it as a singer
in a wedding band, casually

crooning and pointing at the ladies
in the front row. You know, the whole tux
bit: cigarette bobbing between phrases,
diamonds dazzling in the lights, maybe he untucks

his shirt for the big finale. A Tom Jones
sort of deal, big at the Elk's Club and over
at The Riverside. But it doesn't go here, and John,
well, somewhere in that sliver

of brain he's got left is a notion
he picked up after Elvis died: he's convinced
that he's the new Elvis, that the motion
of the stars spilled Presley's spirit into him, evinced

he told me—God knows where these guys
pick up these words—evinced by the fact that he never

could sing a note until the moment Presley died.
But now he wanders through the tables in a fever.

I wish to God I never had to do what I did.
But, like I said, he'd come in and stand at the mike
while the band set up. Most guys let it slide.
Some of the bands know him. Not that they like

the guy. But they understand. Even these young bucks,
they know what war does to a man. But
Johnny, God bless the poor slob, struts
across my bar this night like he's going to explode.

I catch him standing in front of the mirror
in the men's room, practicing some kind of move
with his lower lip. He lets it fall slack, then quivers
his top lip like a cow trying to shake a fly off.

Then he starts twitching like Chaplin doing double time.
Combing his hair in the front window, strumming
an imaginary guitar. Just before showtime
he walks up to me and says—he's humming

"Love Me Tender"—and he stops and says, "Mr. Celentano,
I'd like to sing tonight." That's all he says,
and he walks away through the tables. Then he sits on an
amplifier beside the stage and stares. Just stares.

Not at me, or anyone at all. He just stares. It's like
his eyes aren't seeing anything real. I'm drawing beers,
but I keep an eye on him. I can smell trouble. A fight
in the bar next door will make my nostrils flare.

The guys in the band—it's just a local band, I think
they call themselves *Nightflight*—take the stage
for a sound check. It's funny, now that I think of it—they pick
an Elvis number to warm up with: "Heartbreak Hotel." Strange.

And Johnny takes it as an omen, starts gyrating
his hips and twitching his lip and dancing
across the stage. The guys in the band react funny, letting
Johnny take the mike. He gets his leg flexing,

hunches over and starts singing. And he doesn't sound too bad
at first. A little off-key and he misses his cue on the verse,
but not too bad. When he's done he blows kisses at the crowd—
myself and two bartenders, a couple of barmaids, the regulars—

and walks off like he's just finished a show in Vegas.
I mean the whole deal—waving and bowing and kissing his hands.
It's a little weird, but everyone plays along. It takes us
a while to see what's happening to the guy. By then

it's too late to undo what we've done. He jumps
back onto the stage. I'll never forget how smooth he was,
his black shoes shining, his black slacks, white shirt, jacket slung
over his shoulder. He leaps onto the stage and does,

well, like a pirouette, I guess you'd call it,
and winds up facing the crowd with his knees tucked
together and his head tilted, and he's off—
singing "Hound Dog." I hear my manager say, "We're fucked,"

and I know we're in trouble. Johnny's barking at the mike
while the band watches, amazed. Then he stops singing.
But I spot his toe tapping and realize he's marking
off the solo. He's hearing the guitar, that ringing

lead we all hear when we sing that song in our heads.
Johnny finishes, and the guys applaud again. A few
of the regulars yell encore, but I quiet them with a nod
towards the door. The guitarist buys Johnny a brew,

and lets him sit at his table. I tell the singer
what kind of trouble they're getting
into, but he won't listen. He tells John he's a ringer
for Elvis. He's trying to be nice, but he's setting

a trap for himself. Then I hear Johnny ask a favor
and I know. I feel it right then: trouble.
About ten o'clock the band tunes up. Any later
and I dock them ten percent. Double

for every fifteen after that. It's good business;
the customers know when the music starts at my place.

56

So they play some adolescent love chant, some dizziness
about vans and drugs and a little girl who's the town disgrace.

Same old nonsense. Then I see Johnny weaving through the tables.
He stands to the side of the stage, tall and proud, and right
then I get a little sick. He looks pitiful, like a kid unable
to grow up but wanting to so badly. He stands there. The lights

wash across his face. He slicks his hair back
and coughs into his fist, then stands at attention,
waiting. The band starts another song. It's not "Heartbreak
Hotel." Johnny coughs into his fist again. I can feel the tension

in the audience, wondering who the guy is standing by the stage.
And the band plays, one number after the other. No Elvis,
no Johnny Paris. They look straight ahead, afraid,
I realize, to even look at Johnny, ignoring the promise

they made before the set. I don't know. I've done
the same thing—made promises with all intention
of fulfilling them and then when the time comes,
it's not possible. They finish the set. The singer mentions

something to Johnny as he gets off the stage. Johnny turns
and stands in the doorway, facing the street. His head hangs
forward—like it usually does; then he snaps straight. Stern
and businesslike, he crosses to the bar. He bangs

on the bar—I'd never seen him do that before—
and says, "Mr. Celentano, I was supposed to sing.
They promised." By this time the place is jammed, the dance floor
crowded with kids waiting for the next song.

So I lean close to Johnny and I say, "Maybe another night, John.
The kids want to hear the band." I reach over and touch his shoulder.
But he snaps away. "Mr. Celentano," he says. "They promised on
their word. They said I could sing tonight. I'm getting older,

Mr. Celentano. Give me a chance. My good friend is here tonight.
My good friend Harry Blount. Right over there."
He points to a round-faced little guy. But I've decided.
"Johnny," I say. "The time is not right. Come back another

night." Johnny slaps a glass onto the floor.
He struts between the tables, knocking aside chairs.
He sits on the edge of the stage, sulking. He glares
at the band members. I've got to get him out of there,

even though he's right. Something built-in—like instinct—
decides it, and I take him by the arm and lead him out.
I try to explain, but he won't have it. He stalks
back and forth along the sidewalk, shouting

nonsense. It doesn't even sound like English. It may
have been some language he picked up in the war.
Then the cops come. I don't know who called, but they
grab him, cuff him, and take him away.

I'm not proud of what I did. I still don't know
if I did the right thing. He couldn't sing.
Not like a singer. If he'd had a family, they'd have gone along.
Maybe that's what he needed. Me, I've got this business to run.

The World

"It's a world full of people
waiting for you to fuck up."
My father said that in 1959,
twisting the throttle, one
hand on the suicide shift.
When the phone in the kitchen rang,
my mother's voice was like water
spinning down the drain. We drove
to a warehouse where men in white
worked all night to deliver him
to death, but he did not die.
He became a voice, a wind that
blows through my calm thoughts,
telling me again that the world
waits for you to fuck up,
to splatter yourself against
a bridge or ride over a guardrail
on a mountain road. They'll watch.
They'll pick you up, scrape you up,
load you into a white van.
They'll turn on their lights
as if this were something
to celebrate. They'll make a party
of your demise. They'll run
a photo of your mangled legs,
the half that's left of the motorcycle
that got you there. They'll welcome you
to their heaven of statistics,
talk to your wife on the news.
Some two-bit cop or official
will come on all slicked-up
to tell how stupid you were
to ride without a helmet, as if
the small amount of living we do
in that dark place we call the brain
was something worth protecting.
Listen to what I'm saying.
I come home from eight hours
of picking things up and putting them

back down. I don't go home
to read Russian novels. I don't
play chess with the wife. I ride
to the tavern and drink shots and beers;
I take my bike out on Route Eight,
crack that throttle so wide
my wrist aches. There's something
about speed. It's as if you could
catch up with time, like
if you went fast enough
you couldn't be caught,
couldn't be *seen*. Last night,
past midnight, I felt the tires
flatten against pavement, heard
that silence when everything begins
to glitter, cleansed of sound, cleansed
of the crank and thrust of words
that keep telling it in your ear—
there are limits to what you can do,
as if your body would flake into light,
as if you'd dissolve in the wind,
string out behind like the rap
of the engine, as if your eyes
would press back in your head and see
pain, something pure, more real than this
city of excuses we ride through.

The Furnace Repairman's Wife

I know what a man is: mother
of nothing. That first year
of our marriage, I arched my back
to give him everything. Opened
my body and raised it to him—
lips, hands, the prick
he slid into me like a thermometer.
I know what a man is. Caster
of shadows. Man's got a transistor
at the base of his brain, hears
words direct from God. You see them
drinking in taverns, eating
glass and thrusting their fists
into the smoky air. You see them
in their work shirts and jeans
and you can imagine their
seriousness, all the things
they won't allow themselves.
They fuck with a dull resolve.
They handle their wrenches and couplers
like psalters and chalices,
or hate them altogether,
toss them in greasy boxes.
That first year of my marriage,
whatever pleasure we had flew
like a small yellow bird
up the chimney. On the eve
of our first anniversary
I thawed the cake, sat
in our rented kitchen
in my whitest dress and waited.
Maybe he'd worked late. Maybe
he'd cracked the neck off
a bottle of Jack Daniels
and drank it straight down.
Maybe he stuck his head
into the still warm chamber
of a furnace somewhere
and thought of me. Maybe.

And maybe in that fierce,
hollow privacy, that blackened heart
of some factory or warehouse,
he saw my face momentarily
tipped to receive his lips
and the moonlight. And maybe
a tenderness flensed his flesh
from his bones. But there is a huge gap
between a man and what he does.
Not like a woman. I wore
my scarlet dress into town.
It was our anniversary. Think
what you will. The sign
said *Miller*, and our faces
flushed red as in passion or rage.
He was not a complete stranger;
for nothing, the men teach us,
is complete. He'd wanted me
since high school and now
he had me. But what did he have?
I know what you're thinking:
Good for you. That bastard, your husband,
deserved it. I let that man
turn me and lift me and crush me
and I cried out, feigning
pleasure and rage. He had
another man's wife. Or, to say it
like the men: He was a dog
at another dog's dish. I told him
he was bigger and harder
and better, and he kissed me
as if I were porcelain
and bought me breakfast.
I know what a man is. But when
his gold medallion swung above me,
I thought of sailboats at night,
hundreds of them, moored
in a harbor and the words
halyard and *lanyard* and the silvery
ringing and dull gray knock
and the blue that washed over me
that first night of my husband's love

and how he touched the side
of my eighteen-year-old face
in the moonlight, the canvas
rough against my arm, my face
nestled to his shoulder, his cheek
soft against the top of my head,
both of us looking out
across the rolling bay of our future.
I know what a man is. He sits
in the cab of his run-down body.
He stamps on the pedals, spins
and tugs at the wheel. The body
swerves and chugs, bounces and stalls,
but he gets it done. He's lost
half the load and there's blood
on the fender, but he got it here,
damn it. That's what a man is.

Why I Live on Sutter's Mountain

Here all I remember is failure—
two years lost at school, a buck missed
at fifty yards while dad looked on,
my divorce—as if it happened
in someone else's life. No one
knows me here; or they know me

so recently they can't imagine
my past. My cabin is perched on
granite, surrounded by flowers.
I lose myself in the garden.
Weekends I work out there all day
among gladiolas and tulips.

Breathing like a horse, I root out
weeds, let bone meal filter through my
fingers. Some afternoons I drink
at The Overlook. I sit in back,
stir my gin and tonic, and look
east—Old Saybrook, Connecticut,

the coast, the flimsy bungalow
where we lived one summer. Evenings,
I pack a sandwich and six-pack
and fish the Hudson. I cast for
bass and perch in the shadows of
steel-gray battleships retired from

service and dragged upriver from
Manhattan. Some nights the cadets
come down from West Point with their girls
to shoot the hulls with rifles and
hand guns. In these boys I see my
younger self—life like a series

of walls to punch your fist through. I
plug the river with my spinner.
Bullets hiss, tick the sycamore
leaves. The sounds roll against the ridge,

curve along the angled face like
something alive—a snake of wind

rushing through the grasses. I hear
the cadets above me. I see them
sprawled on the hoods of the hot rods
their parents buy, tossing crushed cans
into the dry weeds. No one knows me
here. If I were to dive and swim

in this dying river, those boys
might fire at me, urged on by their
girls. They won't know what they've ended—
they'll think I'm a bum or a dumb
animal that deserves to die . . .
But there are things worse than death. Like

looking for something nearly dead,
something that won't stand still for the
final blow—the rabbit I hit
while driving Route 82, who
paddled his crushed body into
the blackened weeds while I watched in

the mirror and tried to forget.
But I couldn't forget, and I
couldn't wake the woman who slept
on the seat beside me. There is
enough pain for each of us; there's
no need to share it. Who can we

blame when a rabbit runs under
a tire on a perfect day? Late
last night I woke from a dream
and lifted one hand into the moon
above my chest and stared at it.
I felt my chest, my face, amazed

I lived—that the uneasy truce
the body makes with absence was
unbroken. Such providence leads
me into this sadness, makes me

love this flesh that is not me. (. . . In
Nepal, I've read, relatives eat

chunks of their dead kin's flesh. Down by
a river, where silt glitters like
flakes of skin sloughed off the tall peaks,
where the lammergeiers cast their
simple and frightening shadows,
I imagine the widow of

a good man kneeling to feast on
virtue. *The body is a house*
for terror—tell her that. Goodness
a skin we shed at death, like
stucco on a Mexican church.
Dig deep and find the patchwork of

chicken wire, the rotted planks we're
made of, the hollow where we kneel
to worship, the makeshift altar
where we confuse life and death, where
goats lie down and chickens roost.) If
there is a god let him be as

we are—passing time trying to
make things grow, trying to forget
and remember, to imagine
a world he can bear, waking in
the night, amazed that his house has
not collapsed, that the sunflowers

sway in the garden and do not
break, that the moon soaks them in a
creamy light and is not jerked from
its socket. Tonight while I fished
the Hudson, a storm blew down from
Eagle Crag. The drops fell big and

cold, then it began to hail. I
heard the cars start above me—straight
pipes, glass-pack mufflers rapping. I
reeled my line and sat on the bank,

grateful for the wet and cold. The
battleships creaked in the wind, pulled

at their anchor chains. I sat and
listened until I was soaked and
the sky washed clear. I did not cast
or move. Near dusk, a heron flew
so close I saw the wind luffing
the dark wings, the slight corrections

each feather made. A tiny mouse
slipped between the reeds and skittered
across the taut water. And I
remembered my wife standing
on the porch looking out on a
morning—at the poppies collapsed

from a storm, tulips uplifted
and filled with water. The porch wet,
the hem of her nightgown where it
dragged . . . I remembered and was
saddened by the memory—how
the past is a world filled with friends

where I am always alone. I
remembered my wife telling me
she was happy, and how I would
not believe, could not believe in
a happiness not innocent.
But tonight, at dusk, I stood on

my porch and watched a peregrine
stun a sparrow at the feeder,
lifting it through layers of gray
into an encompassing light
where it was only a black shape.
From inside I heard a woman

talk softly of El Salvador—
men, she said, in wooden crates, mere
breathings behind forbidden doors.
I walked out into the garden,

through gladiolas, sunflowers
looming taller than men, and looked

down to where the moon first lifted
out of the hills. I pulled at a
sunflower stalk. It was like the neck
of the first duck I ever shot,
and, not unhappy, I twisted it
until it loosened and broke.

White Body, Green Moss

I.

South of the river,
on the flood plain
I walk each evening,
cranes lope through saw grass
and blunt-headed fish
rise in murky pools,
the late sun spreads
a thin film of light
across the calming waters
and olive trees gather
the thousand swallows
for the long flight.
There, beneath those trees,
the speaking began:
a voice without location
filled my bones,
yet seemed to rise
from the marrow.
It was a sound so deep
it set bushes ablaze;
mountains lifted and swirled
and faces loomed
until I knew that voice
was the voice of God.

II.

My son was sleeping, the rough white cloth
riddled with shadows as the sun struck
through our only window. I have only known
this impossible world—our burnished sun
rising from its lake of color, the thick wind
that blows all night, the howling wolves
and the deep pond of a woman's flesh.
He was sleeping; I woke him.
His long lashes fluttered like my hands
as I lifted him from the bed,
the bed of burning straw. I thought:

the beast inhabits my eyes, lurks
in the dark between words. And I lifted him,
just six years old, and held him
as he looked out from his dream.
I stood him on the floor; he looked at his feet.
I laced his sandals, and when he spoke
I knew the deed would be done.

III.

While vultures carved their spirals
into winds raised by the sun, its word for *heat*
rising visibly from the sand, we walked.
Near dusk, we reached the mountains
and he dropped onto the cool moss—*his white body*
wrapped in white on the green moss. I turned away,
prayed for strength, unwrapped the knife.
My son slept, his hand draped over his face,
his legs warm and twitching. A fly
hovered over his bare shoulder;
olive leaves shivered with wind, were still.
I raised the knife, and as I did, I looked up
and saw, flying over the single line of black mountains,
two figures, and I heard them call: two violent syllables.
Then they were above us, the two of us—
father and son, and they called again, and again,
the notes I took for words.
                                        Today,
walking south of the river, I remembered those figures—
wide, dusky wings flapping, necks of carved ivory—
and I knew that I had seen the birth of a new language,
new hope for this singular world, a new word for dust,
or sun, or the thick wind that rages all night.
                                                            I placed
the knife on the white cloth, wrapping it slowly.
I did not wake my son; I did not speak.
Now, I no longer hear voices.
I stand beneath the olive trees
and watch the sun plunge into the desert,
and I remember an affliction that seemed an ecstasy,
the knife in my hand uplifted, the white body,
green moss. Even the wind
stilled for my perfect witness.

IV

What are we and whence is
our joy?

—William Blake

The Arena of Civilization

—after Mark Tobey

In Tobey's "Arena of Civilization"
    men and women lounge and work
in a four-tier building beneath a dome
    already invaded by chaos—lines
etched by the imagination or god,
    lines like birds scattering,
fever thoughts, the word repeated
    until emptied of meaning.
In every room of our lives
    a man or woman languishes, or several
conspire around a small table.
    New plans for raising the dome?
The hieroglyphs of purpose remain
    indecipherable. Without a god or some
final goal, what is human striving?

Are these the four tiers
    of the brain? Civilization the dream,
the form that follows man? Or are these
    great men and women not lounging
or conspiring, but sharing wine,
    comforting each other while the dome
collapses and chaos rushes in?
    There is no telling. The petals
of our thoughts unfold, but
    in that scarlet, no answer.
In the falcon's stoop or the merest sigh,
    no balm. Our lives are a web
of small purposes, the stunned rhetoric
    of commerce, fast bucks,
futures, investments. Today

I envied Milton his God,
    the sure touch of his line, the pure
righteousness of each syllable
    creeping heavenward. Or John Donne
in his colloquie, his thought
    "immediate as the odor of a rose."

In Tobey's "Arena of Civilization"
    we live in a small, public building
like clerks unmoved by the brimstone sky.
    Think of Monet, his bourgeois weekends,
boats drawn to the dock, fattened with shadow,
    young lovers gazing out
as they had to at the waters,
    the currents of thin color
pooling in the shade of willows.

Is such intelligence a happy accident?
    Is this the pleasure of death, of life
ending in the pastel present?
    Does civilization rise defiant
towards the shock of whatever hovers
    Platonic behind the sky? Or downward,
trenched deeper against whatever may be true?
    I think of Millet's weed pullers,
how each peasant was pure,
    some focused swatch of sadness
oblivious under the pale sky. How
    as a woman leaned to earth
she knew nothing but the single motion
    required. Required, as a chant
requires a gesture of voice—a falling

in pitch that is neither note nor breath—
    to end. As the guitar loses its notes
in its own black throat; as a thrush
    will swallow its song until
it seems the bird is made of sound.
    Like a carpenter who is a poet,
who is a poet before he is a man,
    as if he must speak himself alive.
Hölderlin wrote, "Man dwells poetically,"
    and Heidegger agreed, who could not force
a song from his tired lungs.
    Like my brother, seven years gone,
whose purpose was the same as mine:
    to contribute some small perfection—
the exact taunt to quicken a room

into life; the cycle shifted hard from third
        to fourth, lofting the front wheel; the switchback
leaned to the edge of traction,
        the kickstand sparking like a meteor.
No god. Perhaps. Or, if so, a god
        who understands wonder, who leans
each corner with us, marvelling
        at the sudden grace of his creations, how
even he was not expecting such beauty:
        porpoises curving silver from the waves,
the gymnast whirling over the pommels,
        the artist taking a knife to the canvas
to carve an ochre room, a man standing
        calmly at its edge while a colorful,
abstract violence batters through the outside walls.

ABOUT THE AUTHOR

JON DAVIS, originally from Orange, Connecticut, currently divides his time between Pawlet, Vermont, and Province-town, Massachusetts. He holds an MFA from the University of Montana, where he won the Academy of American Poets Award and edited *CutBank*. His chapbook *West of New England* received the Merriam Frontier Award, and he is the winner of a 1987 General Electric Award for Younger Writers. He is also the recipient of fellowships from the National Endowment for the Arts and the Fine Arts Work Center in Provincetown, where he currently serves as Writing Program Coordinator. His poetry has been published in *The Georgia Review, Poetry, The Missouri Review, Tendril, Ontario Review,* and many other journals, and a number of his poems have been reprinted in anthologies. *Dangerous Amusements* is his first book.

ONTARIO REVIEW PRESS POETRY SERIES

Jon Davis
Dangerous Amusements
$8.95 paper

Albert Goldbarth
Arts & Sciences
$17.95 cloth/$8.95 paper

Albert Goldbarth
Original Light
New & Selected Poems 1973–1983
$12.95 cloth/$7.95 paper

William Heyen, ed.
The Generation of 2000
Contemporary American Poets
$24.95 cloth/$14.95 paper

Joyce Carol Oates
Invisible Woman
New & Selected Poems 1970–1982
$8.95 paper

Robert Phillips
Personal Accounts
New & Selected Poems 1966–1986
$16.95 cloth/$9.95 paper

Order from Persea Books
225 Lafayette St.
New York, NY 10012